"What is happening now is, you are hearing Kristen's voice over the phone, reading to you in the golden hour when the light gathers before waning. The voice is rough and sweet; maybe if the smell of crushed mint could have a sound, this is the sound it would have. Not even crushed—more like bruised. Barely there. It's a delicate and a complex smell, or sound, or whatever: The meaning is clear and present, always just escaping what you can hold in one indrawn breath. The breath fills you, expands you, wakes you up. You hold it for a moment. And then empty, hold, fill, hold. And repeat. What is happening now is this. This is what is happening now."

—Claudia La Rocco

"Kristen Kosmas's *The People's Republic of Valerie, Living Room Edition* will make the word "undulating" occur to everyone at the same time. And each of these occurrences will take on their own meaning, their own image, their own undulance in the lives of each to whom they occur. This is a work for the living room and for living rooms, the spaces where we are alive and in the company of others.

Through the brief series of monologues that compose this performance text, I find myself alternately leavened and grounded, crushed and revivified by the caring precision of the emotional experiences that weave themselves through the text. Which is to say that, in its generosity of vision and its vision of generosity, it feels real. The novice's (rhymes with Kosmas's) struggle to learn to see and say "what is happening now" as a practice toward ultimately "enacting the Bright Future" is both irreducibly the novice's alone and also ours together."

—Daniel Owen

53sp 34
October 2019
Brooklyn, NY

53rdstatepress.org

The People's Republic of Valerie, Living Room Edition

ISBN Number: 978-0-9978664-3-8
Library of Congress Control Number: 2019948455

Printed in the United States of America

The People's Republic of Valerie, Living Room Edition is made possible by the New York State Council on the Arts with the support of Governor Andrew M. Cuomo and the New York State Legislature.

The People's Republic of Valerie,
Living Room Edition

a play by Kristen Kosmas
with cartography by Leon Finley
& an introduction by Daniel Alexander Jones

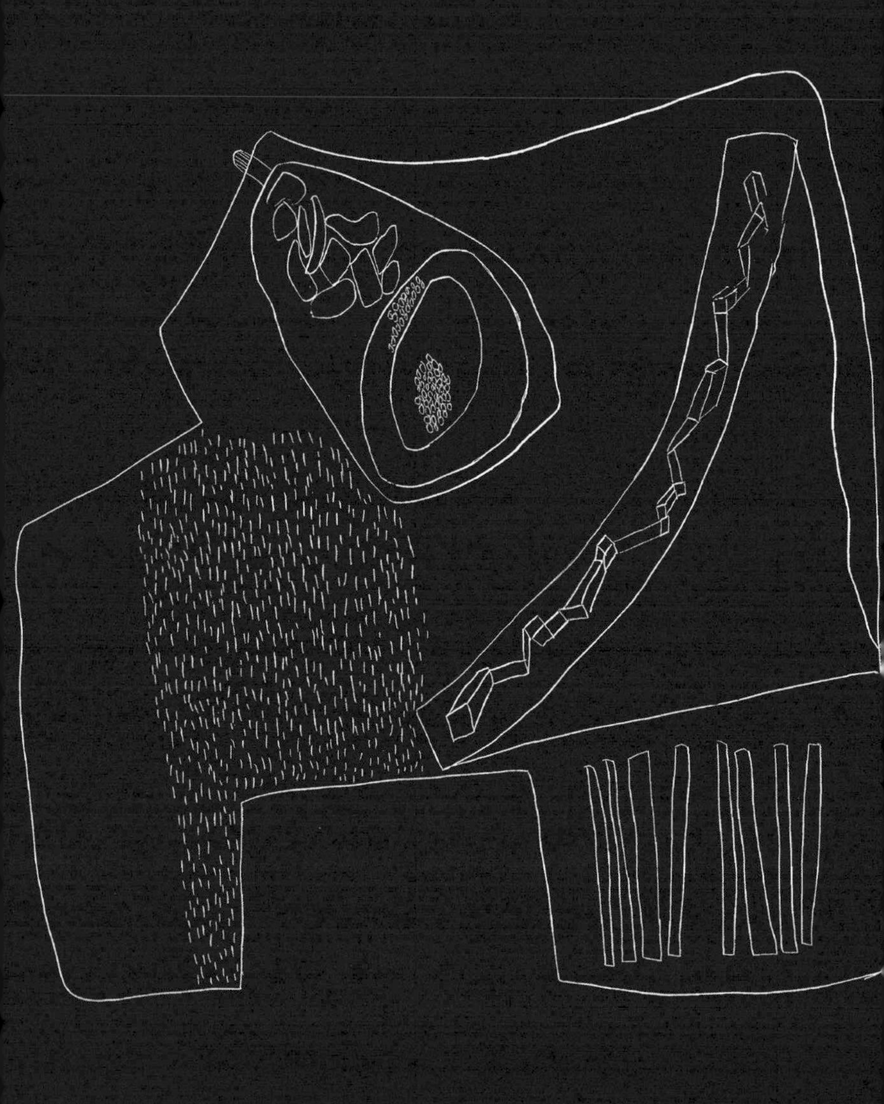

Contents

Preface

Dear Reader,

This is a long story. I hope you will bear with me.

I started writing the text of *The People's Republic of Valerie* in earnest in the summer of 2014. The summer Michael Brown and Eric Garner were killed by police in the U.S., the summer of the Israel-Hamas war, the summer of the rise of ISIS, the summer of the beheading of American journalist James Foley, among others, the summer of the Ukraine-Russia battle and the shooting-down by pro-Russian separatists of a Malaysian airline passenger plane in which 298 people were killed. So far, on our planet, summer still follows spring, and spring of that year included mudslides in Washington state, Chile, and Afghanistan, a tornado in Arkansas, wildfires and drought in California, floods in the Balkans, a ferry sinking in China, and the disappearance of another Malaysian passenger plane, flight 370, in which 239 people are presumed dead.

I had been writing the text already for a while, but I didn't know yet exactly what it was doing or what was going on in it. As far as I could tell at the time, there appeared to be a rather isolated narrator "character" trying to recover or heal from something, but I wasn't sure who they were, and I wasn't sure exactly what was troubling them (which seems absurd now, looking back). I was working at the time quite literally alongside my friend and colleague Tim Smith-Stewart, with whom I'd get together semi-regularly for silent companionable writing sessions. We would sit and write together in silence and then sometimes read and share what we'd done at the end. Tim was writing the text for what would become *Awaiting Oblivion—Temporary Solutions for surviving the dystopian future we find ourselves within at present*, and I was writing what would become *The People's Republic of Valerie*, which would become *The People's Republic of Valerie, Living Room Edition*.

I remember one day after Tim and I had worked together, I think it must have been the day he told me the title of his piece or decided on the title of his piece, I remember I came home and I was sitting outside under this tree and I remember thinking, No more dystopia! No more dystopias! We need a utopia! We need many utopias! And so I began to re-read and re-work—or rather follow and understand—this project toward that end.

It occurred to me fairly soon after making that decision—or after having that idea, or being given that idea (I don't work so much by decision it turns out, more by intuition, or instruction, and an attempt at least at deep listening)—at any rate, it didn't take long after I got the utopia message for me to also get the message that I didn't really know what a utopia was. Nor was I a person yet capable of constructing or imagining one, much less living in one or inviting others to join me in a project that I could barely conceive.

It was clear I had a lot of work to do, and I wasn't sure what it was, but the process of writing this text, and the process of assembling a creative team, organizing a fund-raiser, and rehearsing, producing, presenting, and sharing the play— both at On the Boards in Seattle in May 2017, and afterwards transforming it with my partner, visual artist Leon Finley, to be given in living rooms in Austin, Seattle, Brooklyn, and elsewhere—as well as the process of constructing this book for your use should you wish to use it—has been and is a process of trying to understand what my work is—as a person in this world at this moment—and to do as much of it as I can to the best of my ability.

I continued to work on the text throughout the summer and for the next year and a half with my long-time friend and collaborator Paul Willis and our dear friend and collaborator Peter Ksander. We knew that the show would go up at On the Boards in the spring of 2017, and the three of us or sometimes just Paul and I would meet periodically in LA (where Paul lives), in Portland (where Peter lives and teaches at Reed College), or in Seattle or Walla Walla (where I had dual citizenship during the seven years I taught at Whitman College). Over the years we spent working on the text and trying to understand what it was and how it wanted to be enacted, Paul and I returned many times to the question of whether it needed to be a solo performance or whether it needed to be performed by an ensemble. Because of its theme of the condition of isolation on the one hand, and its aspiration toward or longing for community and collective on the other, we would go back and forth (literally from meeting to meeting) between the two modes. We would meet in LA in the summer and realize the work absolutely had to be a solo show, and then we would meet in Portland in the winter and realize it absolutely had to be performed by an ensemble.

In the fall of 2016, I was making arrangements for my sabbatical from Whitman, during which time I would live in Seattle, finish writing the text, go into rehearsal, and mount the production that was scheduled at On the Boards. Then the 2016 presidential election happened.

I'm just going to pause for a minute to reflect on that event.

And all the events and conditions that led up to it.

And all that has come after.

[ ]

Paul and Peter and I met over the Thanksgiving weekend. We rehearsed. It was hard. We were joined for one day by my friend and colleague Jessica Cerullo (with whom I taught at Whitman from 2012 until I resigned in May 2018—but that is another story). At the end of that work period, Paul was sure that the show needed to be a solo performance, and that was how we agreed to enter the rehearsal room in the spring, although it filled me with dread to think of spending so much time alone. Within two weeks, for a number of reasons, the most beautiful of which (of whom?) was the recently born Augustus Jack Aprile Willis, it turned out that Paul wouldn't be able to direct the show in Seattle after all.

It was swiftly decided that Paul Budraitis, a Seattle director I'd known for many years and with whom I'd crossed paths recently at Whitman where he directed a smart and elegant production of *The Seagull* with students, would enter the process and steward the project to its opening at On the

Boards. I took the opportunity of the change in directors to make an executive decision that we create an ensemble production, and I insisted that we do our best to assemble a creative team that included more female or female-informed than cis-male, more POC than white, and more LGBTQ than straight artists. We didn't achieve this exactly in all areas, but what I learned from even attempting to create a company with this kind of representation has forever changed the way I make and view performance. Our company included, in alphabetical order: Matt Aguayo, Paul Budraitis, Mary Anne Carter, Jessica Cerullo, Leon Finley, Alexandra Harding, Anna Kasabyan, myself, Peter Ksander, Tania Kupczak, Evan Mosher, Brandon J. Simmons, Kelly Morgan Stevens, and Ray Tagavilla. Our rehearsal and design process was challenging and confusing, weird and beautiful, mysterious and rewarding. It's impossible for me to speak of the production because I was in it (and much of the time I was lying on the floor, which was great!), but I've seen pictures. And fragments of video. And everyone's brilliant and essential contributions are present, there, sparkling. And people who saw it still tell me sometimes that the production was meaningful to them, that it did something for them, at that time, in that moment. The show closed on May 7, 2017. *The People's Republic of Valerie* was presented in the same On the Boards season as Tim Smith-Stewart's *Awaiting Oblivion. The PRV*—the work of it, and the work it did on me (and continues to do on me when I have the opportunity to give it again)—owes a great debt to Tim and his project, and to my resistance to the word dystopia. (Although, as it happens, the act and action of his play was more focused on the temporary solutions of its title than it was on the dystopian future we find ourselves within at present.)

I had many feelings after the show closed. Exhaustion, immeasurable gratitude, some great quantity of humility (if humility can be quantified and still be considered humility), depression (as in *the action of lowering something*), and the not uncommon feeling at the apparent end of a massive project that has required an enormous amount of time, energy, labor, and other resources from innumerable humans and several institutions—that something was amiss.

I just looked up the word amiss in the dictionary. It says, *not quite right; inappropriate or out of place*. I love the dictionary.

The thing that was not quite right was that while the production had been meaningful to many, it had still not, as far as I knew, done anything explicitly to change or positively alter or impact any of the crises, circumstances, concerns, or conditions out of which it grew. It occurred to me that if I wanted it to have some direct impact or be of some clear benefit to at least one actual person's actual physical, material life, or at least one place's stability, vitality, reconstruction, or repair, the work might be inappropriate or out of place in a conventional performance setting. I was given another idea: Take it into the living room. Do the solo version in living rooms and give it for free or by donation to raise money for a local organization that is providing relief for people experiencing hunger and/or homelessness.

So that is what we are doing now, more or less, and what we hope you will join us in doing in a living room (or two!) near you, for an organization, community, tract of earth or water, species, or situation that moves you and could use your help in the form of a small donation or simply by boosting the signal of their need.

I'll just say a little more about how the *Living Room Edition* evolved—because it did evolve, and again it evolved with generous input and hospitality from others.

I've known John Kazanjian and Mary Ewald since 1993. I've been a devoted audience member of New City Theater (the independent Seattle company they've been sustaining since 1982), and I've had the privilege of working with them on several projects over the years. I consider John Kazanjian one of my most important mentors (if not my most important) and Mary Ewald one of the country's finest actors. In 1997, I attended their living room production of Wallace Shawn's *The Fever*, directed by John and performed by Mary. In 1990-91, I saw Wallace Shawn perform it at Dixon Place on East 1st Street in NYC and again at La Mama E.T.C. All three of these experiences left an indelible impression on me, and they came to mind as affirmations when I was given the idea to adapt *The People's Republic of Valerie* for living rooms. I reached out to John and Mary, and also to Brandon J. Simmons, to help me think through the idea and determine if it was viable. (In addition to performing in *The PRV* at OtB, Brandon and I had been in a New City production of *Hamlet*—with Mary playing Hamlet—in 2014, so the four of us shared some history, vocabulary, and mutual respect.) We gathered in John and Mary's living room one late summer evening in 2017, and the three of them let me read through the entirety of the text that had been performed at On the Boards. It took about 90 minutes, and they all thought it was viable—though they had some questions! And some suggestions. John agreed to go into rehearsal with me to begin the adaptation process. We met and met and met, worked and worked and worked. It was hard. I struggled again with being alone on stage. Mercifully, I was given another idea.

(If you are still bearing with me, I thank you. I promise I am almost out of ideas! This story, for the purposes I'm telling it to you now, is almost over.)

I met Leon Finley at a Sarah Schulman reading at the Seattle Public Library in January of 2017. He was sitting in front of me, and I noticed that we were nodding emphatically—like, with our whole bodies—at all the same lines from the book (*Conflict is Not Abuse*), and at all the same points in the conversation between Schulman and Mattilda Bernstein Sycamore that followed the reading. Naturally I wanted to meet this person who agreed whole-heartedly, and whole-bodily, with everything I agreed with, so I introduced myself to him after the event and we exchanged contact information. That exchange led to many things, including the *Cartography of The People's Republic of Valerie*, a series of thirty drawings Leon made in response to an audio recording of me saying the text. The drawings were installed in the voms at On the Boards for the audience to encounter as they entered the theater. As I was working with John, and struggling with being the sole performer and focal point of the *PRV, LRE*, it occurred to me to invite Leon to make something for the audience to contemplate with their eyes while I spoke. I didn't know what it would be, only that it should be something simple that could be easily installed in a living room. Leon accepted the invitation.

Meanwhile (I promise it's almost over), my dear friend of

20+ years, Steve Moore, had invited me to do a residency, supported by his theater company Physical Plant, in his backyard shed in Austin, TX, in March 2018. It was my goal to use the residency to memorize the text and return to Seattle ready to rehearse with John and present the *PRV, LRE* at his and Mary's house in May. Leon, by now my partner in art and life, joined me in Austin, where I continued to struggle until I was, finally, given my last idea: Leon should be *in* the *PRV, LRE*, and the visual component should come into being in real time and unfold for the audience in the same way that the audio component (me speaking the text) would. I had some bad ideas about the materials Leon should use to enact this visual component—including an impossible number of green post-it notes—but fortunately for me, Leon is decisive, and attentive, and attuned—to his work as well as my own—and pretty soon (within like 15 minutes of our first rehearsal), he knew that he would draw on an overhead projector using the vocabulary from the *Cartography of The People's Republic of Valerie*. Within an hour of Leon knowing we needed an overhead projector, Steve and his good friend Thomas Graves (of The Rude Mechs, whose space we were rehearsing in) had found and delivered us our dream technology.

As part of the residency, Steve had organized an informal work-share for me with friends from the Austin community. When he asked me what we were planning to do, I said I could share the whole text, which would take about 90 minutes, or I could just share a few sections that would take about an hour. He voted for the hour. So I instinctively (and impulsively) decided to skip two of the six sections that comprised the original text (the two that were giving me the most trouble in rehearsal), and Leon and I set about working on the other four. Instinctively (and impulsively), Leon knew exactly how to adapt the cartography vocabulary for this new iteration of the work, and we haven't looked back or changed it since the first run-through. We gave it for the first time on March 22, 2018, in Steve Moore and Virginia Honig's living room on DeVerne Street.

When we returned to Seattle and began to work again with John Kazanjian (who was totally game to incorporate Leon into our proceedings), it was clear that the piece had a will and a life of its own that had found itself. It would take no further direction! John and Mary invited us (or we maybe invited ourselves) to give the piece again in their living room, which we did on May 25, 2018. Since then, we have given *The PRV, LRE* as a performance duet, for free or by donation to benefit Path with Art, an organization in Seattle that offers free art classes to people coming out of homelessness or recovering from other forms of trauma or addiction. We hope you'll be inspired to do something similar.

We ask only that:

- At least 50% of the donations from your edition go to a non-profit or cause you believe in
- Either you or the good people who are hosting the show provide snacks and drinks (this is what we use the other 50% of the donations for) and make space for socializing for 30 minutes before and 30 minutes after the event
- The event is a collaboration between a Reader/Speaker, a Visual Artist, and the living room they give the work in
- The Reader says all of the words in the script (including

section numbers and titles, such as "Part One, Surveillance"), doesn't memorize them, and doesn't act them*
- The Reader and the Artist are both physically present and co-creating the event live
- The Artist makes or animates something in real time for the audience to contemplate with their eyes— preferably something that is separate and distinct from the bodies of either the Reader or the Artist**

Things we like to do that aren't required are:

- Gather an audience of people who don't all know each other—we like to invite half of the audience and ask the host to invite the other half, more or less
- Send thank you postcards to the good people who hosted the show in their living room/s
- Make the donation to the non-profit or cause in the name/s of the good people who hosted the show in their living room/s

Things we recommend are:

- The Reader uses a music stand
- The Artist sings during the song***

A few notes on the above:

*I wondered for a long time whether I should memorize the text. I asked my friend Joshua Beckman, who had come to one of the editions, what he thought and he said, Definitely not! I said, I think so too! But why? And he said, Because if you're reading it, then it's like something any of us sitting there could do. But if you have it memorized then it becomes about that, about you being able to do that, which most of us couldn't do.

As far as acting goes, it just seems unnecessary here and would only foreclose possibilities. The text itself takes a toll on the Reader because it is long and there is much to move through. Best not to weigh it down with anything extra but just to give yourself to each image, rhythm, and line completely—then move on when you can. Which isn't to say you don't need to rehearse! I recommend it. Highly.

**One of the things that's beautiful about the overhead projector (and the music stand for that matter) is that they are both practical objects that we stand behind. (For the most part we stand behind them.) This has the effect of de-centering us in favor of the audience having a listening and looking experience for their own imaginations. (We're there if they need the work to be about us, but we're not in the way of it being about them. At least, that's the goal.) So it can be nice when the visual component is drawing the eyes away from the Reader and the Artist, though it is possible for the elements to overlap. (For example, during one section in our edition, what Leon is drawing on the overhead is being projected onto my body, onto my clothes and skin, and that's nice too. But it's not necessary. It doesn't need to be projected onto me. It came out of the limitations and the possibilities of the space and the materials we were working with.)

***There is a recording of the song if you'd like to listen to it or use the original melody. But you are welcome to make up your own.

That's it! Thank you so much for your patience and attention. I really appreciate it. And I hope you will use this book. Feel free to contact me if you have any questions. I'm pretty easy to find.

Sincerely,

Kristen Kosmas

Taken Together

(An Introduction to PRV, LRE)

Intimacy has always been Kristen Kosmas's primary medium. In the realm of live performance, of plays, of theatrical events, of public communal contemplations, (however you might name the domain of the experiences she creates), her arterial pulse is profoundly proximate. Indeed, it can sometimes feel as though it were moving right through the meat of you—you who thought you were just coming to observe, but found yourself thrumming in concert. The specificity of Kristen's language, the meticulous crafting of each aspect of the *sui generis* structures of her pieces, and the breathtaking presence of tender, vulnerable bodies (quite often her own) cohere our senses and invite them toward unexpectedly intimate revelation. This exposure, a direct result of her deftly articulated intentions, is communal in scope, but personal in its focus. It amplifies those aspects of our humanity that are collective, while shoring, and honoring, those aspects that are insolubly individual. I've been drawn to Kristen's work for these qualities. Her work affirms my hopes for what live art can do: help us to be more ourselves, help us to be more honestly together, without diminishment or a reduction in the complexity of the whole endeavor. I've marveled at Kristen's work because it accomplishes these things with simplicity, economy, and bravery that feel rare and particular.

In 1996, on a frigid February night in Austin, Texas, at Frontera@Hyde Park Theatre, one of a constellation of small, experimental spaces that threaded across the nation in the early-mid 1990s, I sat in a packed audience for a performance of Kristen's piece, *slip*. It was part of a multiweek festival called FronteraFest that featured a wide range of local artists, plus out-of-towners like me (in from Minneapolis with my piece, *Blood:Shock:Boogie*), and Kristen, in from Seattle. A striking young woman with a vintage coat, beret, and a weathered old-fashioned suitcase entered the otherwise empty space. Light leveled up and Kristen looked at us. Simply, directly, bravely. She didn't look away. She waited. Then she spoke. She conveyed a flurry of images and sensations through sharp, shimmering words and arresting, evolving tableaux. She moved repeatedly from deep interiority outward to that look. Each time she looked out, we saw her differently, as she moved from solid to liquid, from sanity to frenzy, from safety to susceptibility. Each time she looked out she saw us differently, we, changed by the journey she was leading us through. When the lights closed then opened for the curtain call, the air in the room was charged in a way I had rarely experienced. The piece wasn't over although the performance was. Kristen had activated some strange code that would keep unfolding its queries and assertions in my consciousness for the foreseeable future. She had changed us and we knew it.

As I later got to know the self-effacing, keenly prescient person out of whose imagination *slip* had been born, I marveled at the way she embodied all the chewy incongruities of our generation with the potent force of an exposed electrical wire. Sure and unsure, impulsive yet thoughtful, bold yet cautious, and slyly certain that far more was afoot around us than met the eye. I would catch her looking, in everyday life, at all of us. She sensed the subterranean rumblings beneath the supposedly sturdy foundations under our feet, and presaged that they indicated something more true of what our future held than the disaffected, casual gleam and grungy youthful haze distracting us would suggest. She didn't buy what we were being sold.

Our generation. Kristen and I were born within a few months of one another, into the much maligned Generation X. Purportedly we are a swath of unfocused, complaining slackers who have accomplished little and who are viewed as the generational equivalent of lint between the hefty legs of Baby Boomers and Millennials. I've been considering our generation anew, and pushing back on this definition. I see in Kristen's exquisite *People's Republic of Valerie, Living Room Edition* an offering of deep wisdom *from* her as an individual artist with urgent civic concerns, and *through* her, as an exemplar of a perceptive and complicated generational consciousness. She was born into an age of uncertainty and anxiety, and spent her formative years in the uncertain terrain of a nation roiled in the wake of serial assassinations and unfulfilled promises at home as we reached the waning edge of the Civil Rights Movement; shaken by the slow-motion, violent implosion of corrupt American Empire abroad, with the Vietnam War and the Military Industrial Complex's nefarious manipulations of the public trust at the center; and faced with an "energy crisis" that signaled aspects of our current reckoning with climate change. We were in an existential crisis about the direction we would choose, as a country, emerging as we were from the toxic stew of Watergate, other sundry forms of governmental corruption, and a larger societal psychic fatigue. We were facing a bevy of unfinished business and unexamined shadows. (Note: Andreas Killen's book *1973 Nervous Breakdown* provides a useful primer on this time.)

The chosen one arrived on horseback in the form of Ronald

Reagan, whose election initiated a 40-year rightward shift into corporatocracy, deregulation, environmental exploitation, and economic policies that enabled our current staggering income inequality, racialized jingoism and its deadly effects, and the wholesale erosion of rights and protections. A heightened age of uncertainty and anxiety.

Kidnapping and alien abduction were both persistent tropes of the mid-1970s, when we were kids. My mind flashes across a wide range of instances from television cop and superhero shows to movies like *Benji* (1974) about a preternaturally smart stray dog in Texas who thwarts a group of kidnappers that snatch the little siblings who love him. Kidnapping was everywhere. Patty Hearst was in the zeitgeist, and with her the strange contemporary phenomenon of cult kidnapping (body *and* consciousness being taken). The broadcast of *Roots* (1977) laid bare to millions of viewers details of the multi-century institutionalized practice of kidnapping Africans to fuel the nefarious triangular slave trade and build this country. In a strange contemporary complement, alien abduction narratives were also hugely popular. On the one hand, they were the ultimate kidnappings, being taken off the planet to be probed, or tagged, or worse. On the other hand, they suggested a fearsome but potent portal to alternate dimensions, exponentially vast perspectives, and experiences that would forever change the person abducted. In most instances reported, that change was deleterious, eroding any sense of safety, and heightening anxieties. But in some rare cases, abductees reported an increased sense of understanding and purpose.

Last summer, when I sat in a living room in Seattle, among a clutch of polite, but awkward, somewhat random folks gathered together, and proceeded to watch Leon Finley draw his overhead-projected precise circles and lines and shapes with not a mark wasted, as Kristen Kosmas incanted her distinctive phrases, I wondered about inverting kidnapping narratives.

In the piece (spoilers), we are told:

> *"The strangest thing has happened and that is that I have been psychically... kidnapped? I think is the best way to describe it, by an entity, or a person?, or a fantasy, or a person?, called Valerie, who I think is psychically kidnapping, or exiling?, certain, or random, well-meaning but ineffectual people from the planet Earth and "transporting" them, to an asterism called the People's Republic of Valerie where we try to learn, where we aspire, where we train, to remove the in- prefix from the adjective ineffectual which currently so aptly describes us."*

There is another part of growing up in the 1970s that is often thrown out with the critical bathwater. There were genuine attempts by everyday folks across the country to sift through the rubble and, in direct, meaningful fashion, to create some version of MLK, Jr.'s beloved community. Fragments in hand and reaching out across uncertain terrain, we played, we imagined, in order to practice trust or surrender (or however we might name what living an alternative to the isolation and uneasiness might be).

Kristen Kosmas invites our intimate encounter not just with a sober, grown-folks version of such civic possibility, but with her provocation that it will take a radical break from our psychic certainties and behavioral habits to engender the kind of change necessary to both envision and enact a "bright future." Kristen Kosmas speaks to us from a place of wisdom, having identified the granular impacts of decades of anxiety, uncertainty, and deliberate manipulation away from community-mindedness and civic responsibility toward separation, suspicion, and echo-chamber isolation. Kristen Kosmas responds as an artist to the contemporary furies unleashed on the citizenry by inverting the kidnapping narrative. In the shows and movies and stories told back in the day, the emphasis was always on rescuing the kidnapped and getting them home, getting them back to normal. Here, she confronts us with her belief that a return home cannot be a return to where we have been and where we currently are, if "home" rests on collective suffering as its foundation. And that those who have thus far done so can no longer afford to ignore the ways in which "normal" is contingent upon invisibilizing the suffering of others. With *PRV, LRE*, Kristen Kosmas psychically kidnaps us and turns our overwhelmed faces toward the future.

She puts this book in your hands. She asks you to consider performing, presenting, embodying this work (however you might name what you will be doing) and gives you clear guidelines for doing so. It will be an intimate event. You will read her words, and they, by passing through you, will become your words, too. Live visual art will be made in the room with you, opening vistas in front of everyone's eyes in concert with the dimensions revealed by the words. Everyone in the room will be taken. Together.

—Daniel Alexander Jones

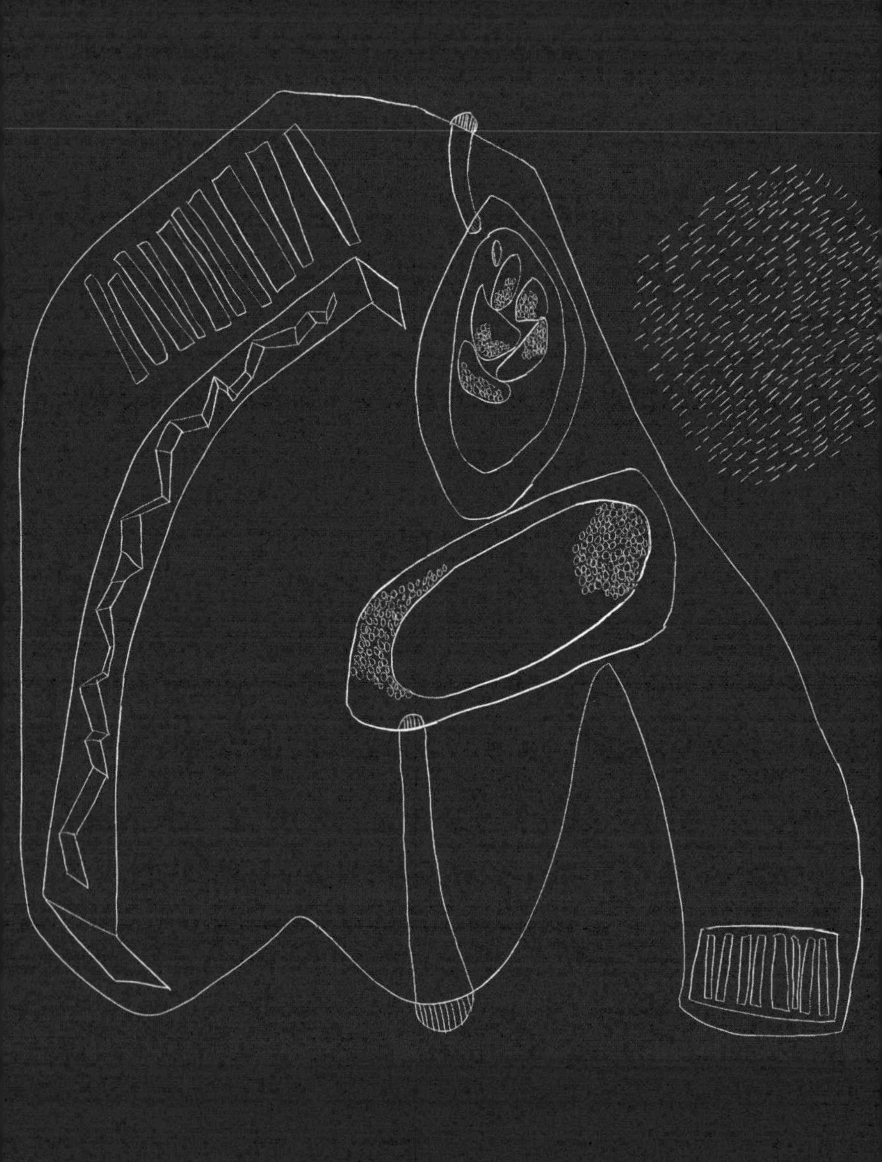

Hello! So
Just a few things before we start.
First,
thank you
so much
(host's name/s)
for organizing this,
and thank you all
for coming
to *The People's Republic of Valerie,*
Living Room Edition.

Uhm . . . The non-living room edition of this show actually has six sections, but
we're just gonna do four of them tonight.

Also,
I want to acknowledge that
some of the lines throughout the text are
echoes, or fragments or phrases, that I borrowed from luminaries and visionaries like Teju Cole, Jill Dolan, Tim Etchells, and also
there are some quotes and images from the dharma and various
buddhist masters.

Uhm . . . also,
we want to just tell you that you can feel free to
look anywhere. You can look at us or you can not look at us, or you can look at the drawings or you can not look at the drawings *(or whatever the visual component of your edition is—slides, puppets, sculptures...)*. You can close your eyes or do whatever you want or need to do with your attention.

It won't distract us, and we won't take it personally if you aren't like—right with us the whole time.

So okay so—

I think that's everything.

So.

The People's Republic of Valerie.

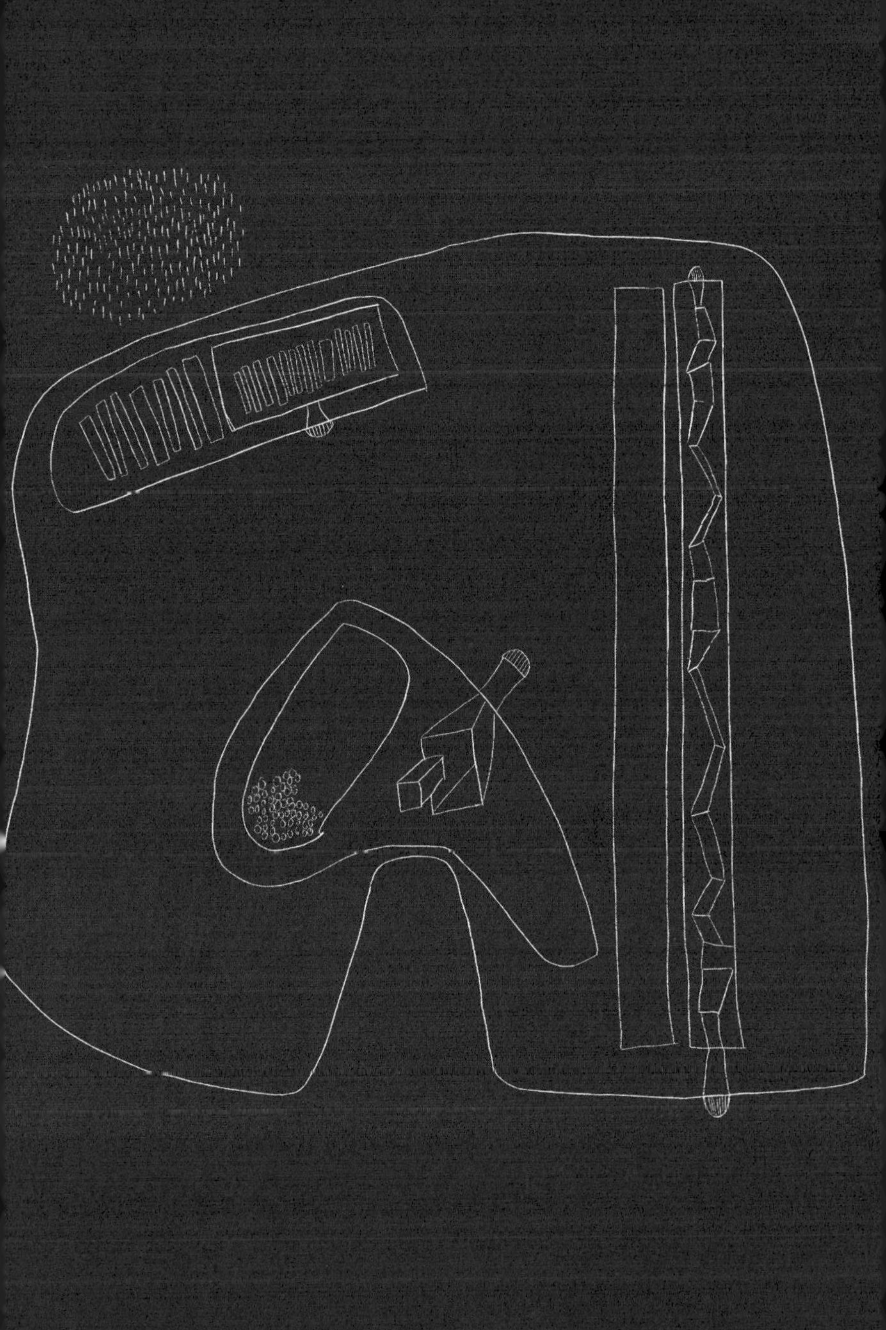

Part One

Surveillance

What is happening is
I am entering
very slowly.
For a long time, you just hear the sound of my
shoes on the floor
while I am entering
very slowly.
When you see me you see that I'm wearing a very…elegant
dress. A formal—a black either evening gown or cocktail dress. It
keeps changing. Sometimes it goes all the way to the floor and
sometimes it's just to the knee. Both versions
are magnificent.

I'm entering.
I'm still entering.

OK I'm…here now, and you notice that I'm holding a tiny plastic
cup of champagne!

The cup is the kind you would take on a picnic if you were
going on a blind picnic date. I'm holding one of those. Where
we are now. Which is here.

There is a soundtrack, a kind of soundscape or soundscore

of a party. Actually, there is a party, now, a whole party, not just the sound of a party, and at the party, there is a record playing. And also there are children, and the children are laughing.

I didn't know children were invited to this party.

What is happening now is
I am wondering whether this is an appropriate dress to wear to a party where children will be present.

What is happening *now* is
someone is saying, You look beautiful.
And I'm saying,
I do?

What happens next is—
Oh. That's hard to explain.
I'm not very advanced yet, so
I'm not even going to try I'll just say that
something very intriguing and very mysterious is happening,
happens
and then I faint.
I have just fainted at a party where children were present.

When someone faints, it is usually because changes in the nervous system and circulatory system cause a temporary drop in the amount of blood reaching the brain. When the blood supply to the brain is decreased, a person loses consciousness and falls over.

That is what has just happened, so now
I'm lying on the grass because now
I'm outside in the yard. It's a yard party, actually.
Or no, actually it's an indoor/outdoor affair. So, while you were able to hear my shoes on the floor in the reenactment of this event in the theater, which is happening now, at the real event, which is also happening now, I entered, passed through the part of the party which is taking place in a beautiful and I presume very expensive house—or home, it might be a home, it's hard to tell, you have to spend a long time in a place to be able to tell something like that. But I heard the record. That was clear. And I heard the children. They were clear. And you heard my shoes as I entered the party and the theater in the magnificent dress of indeterminate length.

At some point, I was handed a tiny plastic cup of champagne by a gentle
person with whom it seems likely that I will eventually go on a blind picnic date, and they
said I looked beautiful and I said, I do? and then I passed through the sliding glass doors to the outside yard part of the party where I was standing on the grass when the mysterious thing happened before I lost consciousness and fell over.

So what is happening now is I am lying on the grass.
And I am not moving.
And my body is in a kind of horrible position.
It's a horrible position to be in.

It's kind of like—
No. I don't know how to do it. You'll—
You'll just have to imagine it.

OK so I'm lying there next to the little plastic cup of spilled champagne
and my eyes are opening
and there is something glimmering
in the corner of my eye, out of the corner of my eye
(which is a horrible phrase)
Anyway there is something…gleaming?
over there and I wonder whether anyone else can see it. Is there—water over there, or
a mirror or, a tiny, magical creature fluttering about and reflecting the light? There's light shining through or bouncing off something over there. Can anyone else see that?

I'm lying there.

I'm still lying there.

Now a young man named Tim is entering and he is offering to help me up and I'm saying no.
I say, No. It's OK.
Tim is, and maybe you are, wondering whether it's really OK
or whether I'm just trying to be nonchalant,
whether I'm just trying to be not humiliated
down there.

None of us is quite sure.
None of us is ever quite sure.
Or, we are rarely quite sure. Sometimes, rarely, we are quite sure, but this is not one of those rare occasions, and even on those rare occasions sometimes we have turned out to be wrong.

Anyway Tim decides to help me up anyway and secretly I am grateful.

Oh. But now another version is happening where he enters, offers to help, I decline, and he walks away,
leaving me in the horrible position. In this version, everyone is wondering whether they have made the right choice, the merciful choice. We won't know for a while yet.

In yet another version,
the one which is happening
NOW
no one enters, no one offers to help, and there is no young man named Tim.
This is the most unfortunate version, and it is unfortunately the one that is happening…
now.

Almost all of the time
I am just trying
to be not humiliated.

At some point, I will climb into the ceiling.
But not now.
Or no.
It is now. I just climbed into the ceiling. I got up off the grass and climbed into the ceiling now.
Sometimes I get shy.

OK *now* something is happening that doesn't have anything to do with me!

What is happening now is
everyone is seeing something beautiful in nature.
Everyone at the party where I fainted in the grass
and everyone here, in the theater, is now simultaneously
observing an act
or fact
of nature. What it is is—
It is tall yellow grasses blowing in a gentle breeze. There is a perfect blue sky above and three, perfect white clouds in the perfect blue sky.
Everyone sighs and calms down immediately and instinctively.

Now there is a close-up, of just the grass, moving, in the breeze. It looks like kind of a sea, the way it is moving. The word *undulating* occurs to everyone at the same time. All at once the word *undulating* comes into the mind of everyone simultaneously and everyone feels a tiny sense of pride at having found the right word, at having located the perfect word, especially since

it is a word that everyone does not use very often and so it has
that special magical feeling, that special magical quality that
being articulate can have, that being articulate
presumably has.

The breeze picks up suddenly, and the sun comes out from
behind one of the clouds, and so the
light it—
the grass it—
and the undulating it—
comes to a kind of crescendo, and everyone
stands, and everyone
applauds, and everyone says,
Beautiful! Just beautiful! Extraordinary!
Everyone says, Perfection! Absolute perfection!
They give the grass a standing ovation.

I however am not clapping.
I am not thinking, Perfection!
I am thinking, God damn it.
And I am throwing one of my shoes at the wall
and it is landing on the floor
with a dull thud.

OK, now I'm eating a cracker.

I'm still lying on the grass of the mental theater where I have fainted in the side yard of a party where there are children present and a record is playing. I'm still wearing the beautiful black dress that may or may not be inappropriate for a party where children are present. (At this point, the dress appears to be knee-length.) My legs and arms are splayed out in a horrible way. I believe I mentioned that. And just now, the person who told me I looked beautiful before has come over and knelt down on the grass beside me and righted my tiny plastic cup, which dropped when I fell and spilled. They came over, set the cup upright, and walked away.

Or no. They set the cup upright and gave me a cracker.

Or no. It is not the person who thinks I look beautiful. It is Tim who is setting the cup upright and giving me the cracker. The person who thinks I look beautiful, it turns out, wasn't invited to this party, which is probably for the best, because even though I was hoping to see them, I'm relieved that they are not seeing me in this position.

Tim has brought me a cracker.

Or no. Nope! Sorry. What is happening is that I have the crackers in the pocket of my dress and I'm getting them out now and unwrapping them and eating one. Peanut butter. I hate to say it, but they're peanut butter crackers. Apparently, I'm the kind of person who takes her own snacks to parties just in case. The peanut butter crackers are wrapped in plastic and the plastic is making a lot of noise in what is otherwise a silent scene.

Now, there are scenes that I'm not in.

I wonder what is my part in, or relationship to, scenes I'm not in.
I'm a novice. So I won't know for a while yet.

The scenes include but are not limited to a herd of rhinoceroses and a first aid kit.
They include but are not limited to a cake plate falling off a shelf and shattering.
They include but are not limited to an earthquake resulting in the deaths of—
A tidal wave resulting in the deaths—
A lunar eclipse—
harming no one.
A solar eclipse
blinding several.
A woman—
A fire—
A child—
A boating accident—
but everyone is all right. Or we think everyone is all right, but we won't know for a while yet.
Now it is getting dark.
Now it is getting light.
Now it is getting dark.
It is getting light.
It's getting dark.
It's getting light.

Now there is music, instrumental, and I am laying sod
in the theater
which is where we are now.

Other things that are happening are:

A middle-aged white woman is standing on a sidewalk. She looks down and sees a button in the dirt in one of the cracks in the sidewalk. She is considering picking it up. She is wondering what it fell off of.
A middle-aged Latina woman is relearning the definition of the word *reification*.
A black woman, probably in her sixties, is considering the process by which human beings become dominated by things and become more thing-like themselves.
A young... white ...cis-male person is
reading the following quote on a bathroom wall: The future will be confusing.
But the quote is written backwards, so the young person has to read it in a mirror.
An older gentleman, I think Armenian but some argue African American, is writing something on a bathroom wall. I can't read it yet. I don't know yet
the alphabet
he is using.

A Russian woman, mid-sixties, is whispering terms of endearment to her cat.

A Japanese cartographer is collaborating with a German poet
on a land-art project involving olive trees in Italy.
A white woman in her late thirties is
learning how to drive
A black man in his…mid-thirties is…thinking about his laundry.
He's in his bed by the window. He's looking out the window but
he's not really seeing anything. Or no—
he is seeing
three perfect white clouds floating by.

A young white woman is—
A young white woman is…
terminating a pregnancy. A Syrian woman in her early forties is
having a baby. A trans man is
carrying a child to term! He's in his third trimester.

Now there are walls
Now there are lamps
Now there are candles
Bears
Deer
Moose
shedding their antlers
Now there is a bird
In a cage
Now there is a bird
not in a cage

A father is dying

A father is dying

A father is dying

A father is dying

A mother is grieving
A mother is—apologizing
A grandmother is
installing a light fixture, planting
a tree, translating
a novel, burying
her mother
consoling
her son
burying
her son
consoling
her daughter
A grandfather is
planting a garden.

OK now a couch
is bursting into flames
center stage!
Everything a couch!

center stage! represents!
is bursting into flames!

Oh. Now you
are standing on a bridge
spanning a big river.
Your skin is vibrating.
Your cells are vibrating.
You are forgiving someone
who doesn't even know you're mad.

Now someone is carrying someone else through an emergency
in a wheelbarrow.
Someone is moving toward a silent vigil.
Someone in Uganda is being put in an ambulance.
Someone in Uruguay is getting married.
Someone in India is
taking his vows and donning his robes while his brother, else-
where, is falling in love.

Now someone, somewhere is saying, It echoes in here.
So if you shout, it keeps happening.
So we don't shout in here.
So please don't shout in here.

Now, the party is over.

And I have laid all the sod.
And I am lying on it in the theater, which is where we are now.
At this point,
three clouds float by and have a conversation.

The first cloud is saying, Make a right! No, a right, a right!
The second cloud is saying, To the right is an ocean.
The first cloud is saying, Yes! Yes, I want to go there! To the ocean!
The third cloud is saying, To the left is a river.
The first cloud is saying, I want to go to the ocean, the ocean!
The second cloud is saying, Did you know
that at a certain time of year
there is only one kind of fish in the river?
The first cloud is saying, The ocean! I want to go to the ocean,
the ocean!
The second cloud is saying, I'm just saying.

The clouds go on and on like that.
It's not very interesting.
They're not very interesting clouds.
Perhaps they have relied too much on their beauty.

Oh. Now the third cloud is saying, Hey.
It is saying, Uh oh, hey.
It is saying, Hey
do you guys see that boat?
It is saying, That boat
is headed for some danger.

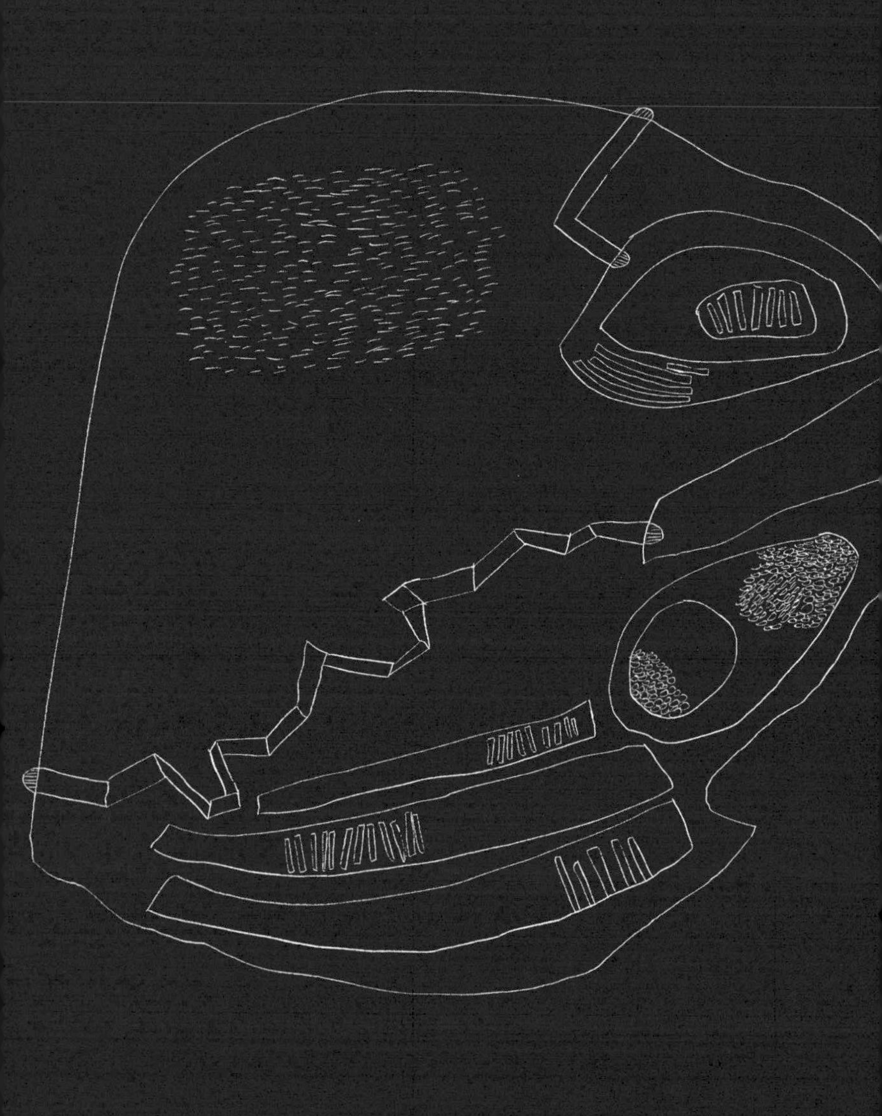

Okay so
we're gonna skip the next section,
which is Part Two, Part One,
and it's called Training Ground, or
Where We Are Now
and basically what happens in that section is that The Novice
(refer to self)
wakes up
with a motley assortment of other well meaning but ineffectual people *(refer to audience)*
on an asterism *(refer to space)*
called The People's Republic of Valerie
where they all get
bossed around by a benevolent
dominatrix nurse, basically
is what happens
but

I'm just going to read the last page
of that section

and then we'll go on.

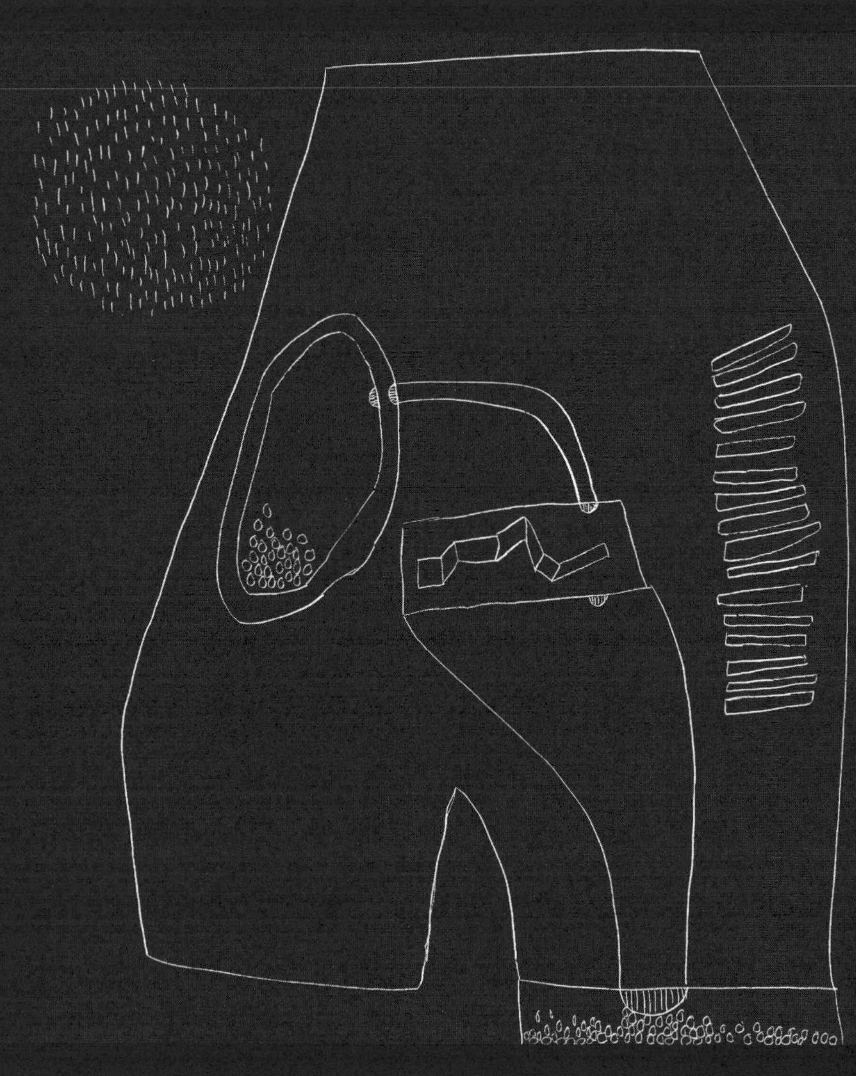

Last Page

Part Two, Part One

What is happening now is
We are going to bed, and the Nurse
is getting a beer from the refrigerator.
She is taking off her remarkable shoes and unbuttoning her tight white dress down to here. She is taking off her tight white dress and throwing it over the back of the chair and sitting in the chair in her underthings. The wooden chair, in the office, by the wooden desk, by the window. She is drinking the beer. Very slowly. And she is saying,

> The thing is
> they were not all that well trained. Here, they work
> toward an accurate general sense of everything.
> They learn
> how to be a rock in order someday
> to be a tree. Or a flower. Or wind or lightning or a typhoon. According to their nature.
> But first, they have to learn
> how to be a rock.
> Eventually, some of them will learn
> how to be invisible in places. In parts. They will learn how to have invisible parts and some of them, if they are a peacock, might learn how to swallow poison, and let it make their tail feathers more sleek, more brilliant.
> Some of you may learn

to swallow fire,
to shoot arrows from your ears, to see
what is hidden with your so-called lazy eye
while your other eye sees
what is apparent.
Some of you will learn
the new surveillance,
how to see
and say
what is happening now.
Because if you can see things as they are,
then you might be able to see things as they should be.

Someone says OK no but seriously.
Where *ARE* we?

The Nurse
doesn't answer.

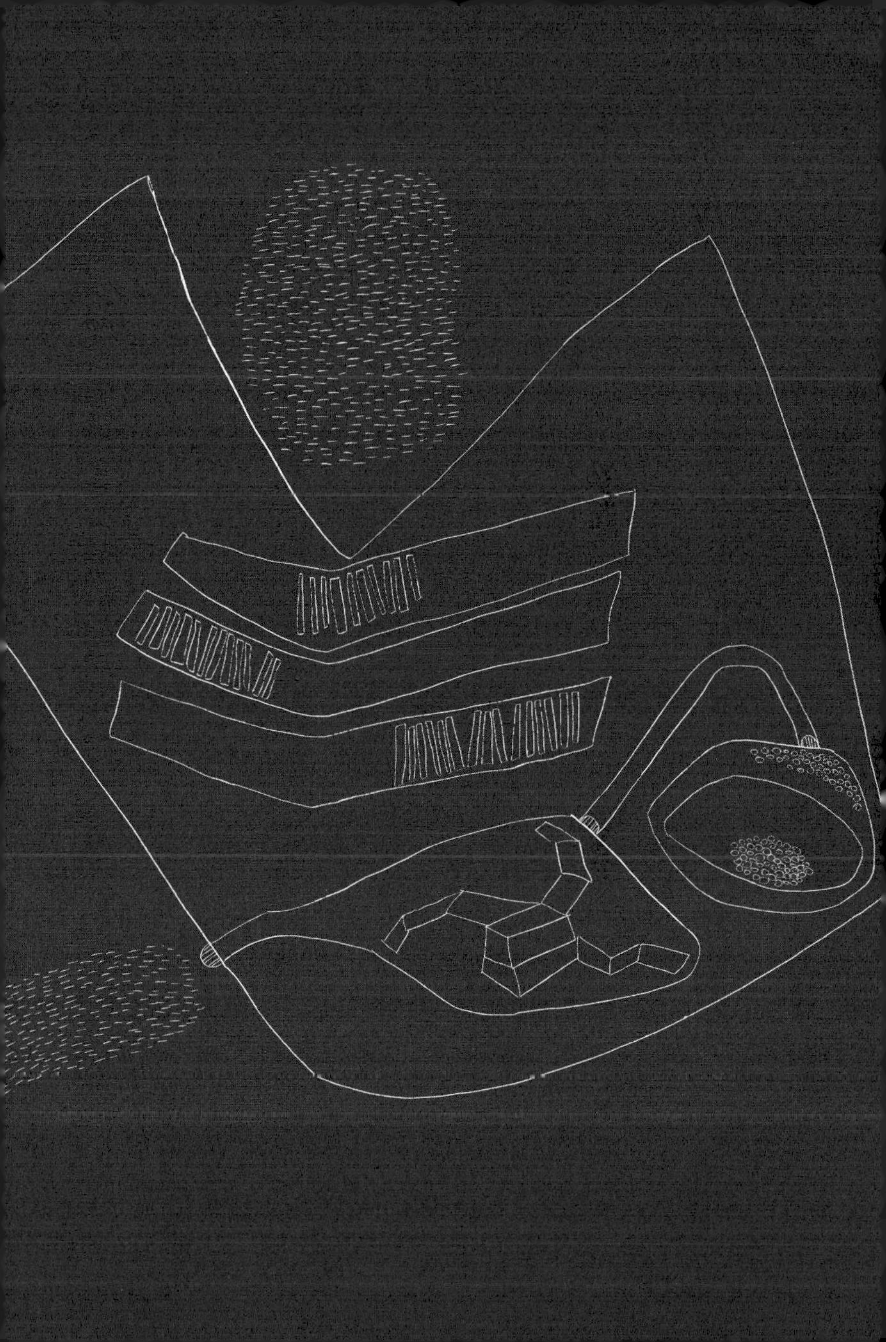

Part Two, Part Two

How It Happens

How it happens is
one minute you'll be like—
Or you'll be like—

Or you'll be like
eating a cupcake
a whole cupcake
in one bite
Or you'll be like
pounding on the earth with your fists and cursing at the sky
with your voice
Or you'll be like
pounding on your own flesh with your fists and cursing the day
you were born with your voice,
Fuck You November Sixteenth Nineteen Sixty-Nine (*or insert
your own birthday here*)! Fuck. You.
Or you'll be like
lying in bed with your head on a pillow and tears will just be
pouring out of your eyes, pouring, tears will just be like
pouring out of your eyes and pooling into your ears and spilling
out and over and onto the pillow and you'll be like,
begging
or praying or whatever.

Or you'll be like lying on the floor under a
window in the ceiling,
a *skylight*, with your head on a shoe and you'll be watching
airplanes fly over and you'll be like, *Flight path. Flight path.*
And you'll be like
unbuttoning your shirt to show the airplanes how you have SOS
written in giant letters in permanent marker on your stomach
and you'll be like
hoping someone in the airplane will see
and that they'll parachute
out of the airplane and land
perfectly and gently on the roof of the abandoned building
you're taking a nap in while you're on a fifteen-minute break
from work.
And they'll open the window in the ceiling you're lying under,
they'll open the *skylight*, and they'll like
rappel noiselessly down the wall and come over to you and
bundle you up and somehow attach you to them with like
straps and carabiners and then
A rope comes down from out of the sky and the person grabs
onto it with one hand and keeps hold of you with the other
and the two of you rise up and out of the building and out of
your job and out of your life and out of this city which is in this
state which is in this country which is almost unimaginable
except from great heights.

Or you'll be like
making a documentary on your phone of a snail.

Of a snail, snailing away from your front door, across your welcome mat on your porch and down the steps and away down the path and you'll be like
trying to decide what you should call it,
the documentary.
Thanks For Stopping By or
See You Next Time or
Sorry to See You Escar-Go.

Or you'll be sitting in a chair with your hands on your head like this.
Or you'll be standing at the kitchen sink holding a glass in your hand
getting a glass of water but the water will be like
running and running
and you'll just be—

And that's when maybe it will happen.

Or maybe when you're like
giving five dollars to the schizophrenic man at the 7-11 who's telling you about the holes
they drilled
into his head, how they kept—
how they still have part of his skull there at the hospital, how they're keeping it there in a jar and they won't give it back.
It might happen then.

Or it might happen when you're washing your hair.

Or rearranging the rocks in your yard.

Or it could happen when you're—

singing.

Or when someone's like, Hey, How's it goin?
and it takes you like 56 or 57 minutes to respond
during which time you get completely derailed on several profoundly neurotic tangents before you finally
realize and say,
I'm sorry, what was the question?
And they say, Yeah, just like,
How's it goin?

Or when you're
turning off your phone or not opening any of your mail or not
eating or eating everything in the house
Or when you're turning off all the lights and closing all the
curtains and pretending you're not home, even to yourself,
and when you're like, Dude. I know you're here. Obviously you
can't—*I*—am always gonna know—*you* are here. And you're like,
Fuck You November Sixteenth Nineteen-Sixty Nine (*or insert
your own birthday here*).

Or when you're
standing over something

standing over something looking down at it
and you're like, That thing is broken.
That thing is totally broken and it's my fault
And it wasn't even my thing
but I was responsible for it for like
five minutes during which time
it got broken.

Or when you're like
washing the windows
or scrubbing the floors
or taking out the garbage
or doing the laundry
or taking out the recycling
or doing the laundry
or taking out the garbage
or cleaning out the refrigerator
or washing the floors
or taking out the garbage
or doing the laundry
or washing the windows
or sweeping the floors
or shaking out the rugs
or ironing the curtains
or washing the curtains
or taking down the curtains
or sweeping out the garage
or taking out the garbage

or taking out the recycling
or making the bed
or making the bed
or making the bed
or making the bed
or washing the windows
or dusting the figurines
at somebody else's house
or scrubbing the bathtub
or mopping the ceiling or
vacuuming the roof or
ironing the grass or
mowing the couch or
sharpening the scissors or
changing the oil in your dresses or
fluffing up the windshield of your
car or
shaking out the rugs or
cleaning out the basement or
cleaning out the attic or
cleaning out the closet or
cleaning out the cabinets or
climbing in the cabinets or
hiding in the closet or
sleeping in the attic or
living in the basement

Or

When you're not doing any of those things
When you can't do any of those things
It could happen then too

It could happen
any time

One minute
you'll just be like
doing something
Or not doing something

But you'll be a certain kind of person

You'll be a certain kind of person who is there

You'll be a certain kind of person who is there one minute
Doing or not doing something
And then the next minute

You'll be gone

You'll just be
gone

You'll just be gone

You'll just be gone

There's a flash,
a blaze a
coruscate
Then there's a
dis-integration a
shattering a
splintering a
smithereening

It sounds terrible, and it is
kind of terrible
It's complete physical
rack and ruin

But it's also kind of beautiful
Especially in your memory
It's like
if you were made of glitter
If you were made of seven billion billion billion—that's a 7
followed by 27 zeros, if you can imagine—
It's like if you were made of seven billion billion billion pieces of
glitter
And they all blew apart all at once and were all scattered
Into the air

It's like if you erupted
Into seven billion billion billion
pieces of light and were broadcast

and dispersed
Or first dispersed
and then broadcast
Dispersed
for a long time first
And then broadcast into something like

a little boat

Or like a ship's container but it's not made of any
material substance it's just—
Fuck I don't know what it is it's like an idea
But it's real
But it's not physical
But it has a shape
And it's sort of the shape of a boat
And it's sort of the shape of a ship's container
Or wait
Ffffffffggghhhhaaaa
It doesn't have a shape
It just has a feeling
Of a place you've never been before, i.e., a ship's container
But that you can imagine, i.e., a ship's container
And that serves a purpose, i.e., a little boat
Which is i.e. familiar and has i.e. a purpose of transport

But it's all happening in slow motion like

ppppppqqqqqqqqqqqqqqqqqqqqqqqqqqqqqqqqqqq
qqqwwwhhhwwwhhhhwwwhhhhwwwwhhhhhhhhh-
huuuuuuuuuaaaaaaaaaahhhhhhhhhhhhhhhhh

(*Ideally, this sound should be made on one long out-breath and it should take about 25 to 40 seconds and be accompanied by a long, slow gesture with the hands.*)

That's how you get there.
To The People's Republic of Valerie.

While you are dis-integrated
Or still in your erupting
glitter state
On, or in, or being held or transported through—
Pieces of your pieces, let's say seven billion of your seven billion billion billion—which is roughly, what?, a third?—roughly a linguistic third of your independent, shining atoms have some… consciousness. That's not right. I know that's not right, but let's call it that
for the moment.
Your…consciousness, roughly a third of your…potential
is aware
that there are other billion billion billions being transported with you.

Are you following me?
Doesn't matter.

You realize
" " realize
You "realize"
that you are not alone,
and that you are not whole.

That isn't a metaphor.
Oh that's funny. That sounds like a metaphor. That isn't a metaphor.
I mean
it's not a metaphor
for the *larger* story I'm trying to tell you.

Anyway so yeah so then *also* all at once but *also* in slow motion
your seven billion billion billion independent shining atoms
magnetize, and find and draw back toward one another and
coalesce
again, reconstitute
here
in more or less the shape of your person
(I think some of my weight got
redistributed, but—)
More or less you
cohere
again
here
particle by sparkling particle
on The People's Republic of Valerie,
an asterism

composed of stars
from more than one
constellation.

You regain consciousness
simultaneous with your cohort
You wake up
All scattered on the strand.

> In astronomy, an asterism is a pattern of stars recognized in the Earth's night sky.
> Like constellations, asterisms are, in most cases, composed of stars, which, although visible in the same general area, are often located at very different distances from Earth.
> Simple shapes composed of a few stars make asterisms easy to identify. Thus, they are particularly useful to people who are familiarizing themselves with the night sky.
> Which is what most of you were doing
> consciously or not
> metaphorically or not
> because you have insomnia or not
> before you arrived here. You
> were familiarizing yourselves
> with the night sky,

The Nurse tells us.

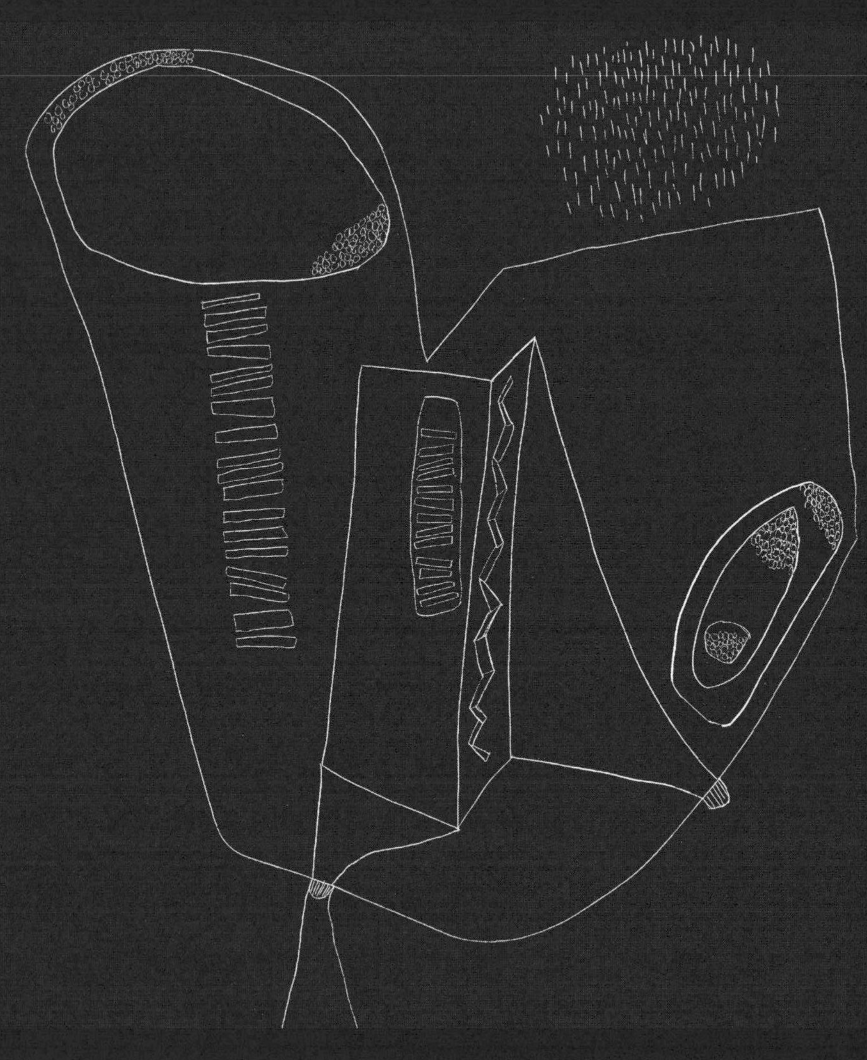

Part Two, Part Three

You Get One Letter

Dear Dan,

I'm so happy I got to see you recently because it looks like I am not going to be able to see you again for a while.

The strangest thing has happened and that is that I have been psychically... kidnapped? I think is the best way to describe it, by an entity, or a person?, or a fantasy, or a person?, called Valerie, who I think is psychically kidnapping, or exiling?, certain, or random, well-meaning but ineffectual people from the planet Earth and "transporting" them, to an asterism called the People's Republic of Valerie where we try to learn, where we aspire, where we train, to remove the in- prefix from the adjective ineffectual which currently so aptly describes us.

I am not alone here, which is wonderful, because as you know I was very alone where I was before. So while this sudden and mysterious relocation without warning is... inconvenient in some ways (although frankly not that many), it is also kind of excellent in other ways although often it is also horrible and amazing.

I don't know how long I'll be here. I don't know how long I've been here. We get to write one letter. Like how in prison you get one phone call? Here, we get one letter, and I hope it's okay that I'm writing mine to you.

Part of me thinks they won't actually deliver the letter anyway.

When I was in my twenties, I had this great boyfriend who took me to the hospital once, when I had to get my wisdom teeth pulled. And I remember, when they put me under, before they pulled my *wisdom* teeth, they had me count backwards from a hundred while the anesthesia took effect.
As I was counting backwards from a hundred, I remembered
how dangerous anesthesia is, and I remembered
how some people never come out of it, anesthesia, and I remembered
that that's why anesthesiologists get paid so much money.
Because some people never come out of it.
Naturally I panicked remembering this and I thought, Obviously I am not going to come out of it, I am obviously going to be one of the ones who doesn't come out of it! And so naturally I wanted to see my boyfriend again, one last time, before I went under, and never came up.
So I asked the nurse, I said, Can you get my boyfriend, please, just for a minute? I just want to see my boyfriend again for a minute before I—
And the nurse goes, Sure. We'll get your boyfriend.
And even though I was almost already entirely under at that point,
I *could* still discern tone of voice, and I knew
She wasn't gettin' my boyfriend.

And the last thing I thought before it all went dark,
which could have been the last thing I *ever* thought was,
Liar! You're a liar!

Anyway I did come out of it, obviously, and my boyfriend was right there next to me, with his crazy hair, and his goofy smile…He was a really good boyfriend. We were gonna have a sunflower farm together when we grew up. God we were young.

Anyway I think this one letter thing might be the same as the anesthesia thing. Like they're like, Sure we'll send this letter to your friend Dan. And then they throw it in a furnace.
But I am writing it anyway
because who knows?

Anyway.

How are things there?
Is it still the same?
Is the world still trembling?
Is there still fire
falling? Meteors? Boulders of fire
falling from the sky, is it still raining fire?
And people's mouths? Is there still spontaneous
bleeding occurring and are people still
threatening each other with rocks and in
some cases using them?

Are people still speeding and is their speeding still causing
more and more speeding and a great deal of nearly colliding?
Are cupcakes still popular?
Are people still falling into holes? Large and small holes in the
earth, is there still a great swallowing?
Are there still clouds? Tremendous clouds, something beyond
clouds where the clouds belong? *Like* clouds but like mountains of
clouds and are the clouds still made of filth and the color of filth?
Are there still animals? Is that thing still wrong with their eyes
where their eyes have been replaced by wheels?
Are people still having children?
Are people still dressing their children up like frogs and bugs
and parading them around like showdogs?
Are people still dressing their dogs up like equestrians and
pushing them around in strollers and carrying them in purses?
Are there still dogs dressed up like cops patrolling the airports?
Are there still dogs that are cops on leashes?
Are there still people dressed up like cops patrolling the cities
and the airports with the dogs and the people on leashes?
Are they still keeping all the art in one building?
Are there still bagels? Fountains? Statues? Prayers? More impor-
tantly,
are you still on Grindr? Or Tinder? Or both?
I hope not.
Because that might mean—
Well that could mean so many things
but it might mean
that you found someone.

I looked up the prefix in- in the dictionary. There were two
definitions.
When I say that here we are training to remove the in- from the
ineffectual,
I believe we are training to remove the in- 1, not the in- 2.
The in- 1 is the one that means not, without, lacking. As in
inanimate, intolerant.
The in- 2 is the one that means toward, within. As in
include, incandesce.
I hope you are not removing your in- 2.
I hope you are not on Grindr
or Tinder anymore because I hope that you are
moving toward and/or within someone. I hope you have found
someone to include and
within whom
to incandesce.

In addition to shedding the in- from my effectual
my particular training here is also in the new surveillance,
which has to do with observing,
with learning how to see
and say
what is happening now.
Eventually, I am told, I will also learn how to remember correctly, but right now
I am a novice and that is apparently advanced work for the
future. Until I advance, I am discouraged

from remembering at all. This is really hard, Dan. For example, I
remember you often. But now I wonder
if I remember you correctly.

I wish you could write me back.

The other day they told us that if we needed anyone we could put our names on a list and someone would come and find us and we could talk about it.
I totally put my name on that list.
I totally need someone.
They haven't come yet.

Dan.
Remember in Orlando—
Not the city,
though the June 12th, 2016 tragedy there
and others like it in other places are and have been *ACUTELY* on my mind—
But remember in *Orlando* the book by Virginia Woolf, remember when Orlando spends a hundred years alone under an oak tree with their dogs, forsaking human company in favor of solitude and contemplation of nature? (At least, that's how I remember it.) But you know how we're all so isolated these days, so despondent and dolorous, and you know how we have been for quite a while now and how no one knows where to place the beginning of this…anthropological age, this…geo-illogical age?

I remember when I read *Orlando* the first time and I got to that century of their life.
I remember I was comforted. Because I thought, I'm in that century of my life too. Alone. Under a tree. And so are you. Y'know? So are you.
But I thought, It's okay. We are all alone sometimes. And far away. For a hundred years. It's okay.
And it is from that wretched and blessed (*pronounced "blesid"*)
century of ours
that I write to you now.

Even though I don't think you will get this,
I think somehow you will get this.
They say, Sure. We'll send this letter to your friend Dan. Then they throw it in a furnace. Up here. But maybe it rains down on you, down there, like some strange
paranormal ash, some weird…supernatural ash.

I can see you
on your fire escape
looking up
receiving it.
A fine dust collecting
on your hair, in your beard, on your sleeves. You're smiling.
And that's me. That dust, that's these words. But better. 'Cause they're just an element now, they're just elemental now. That dust is these words. Settling on you. And even if you don't know exactly what it is, I like to think that you know

exactly what it is.

I wrote this song today.
There's a person in my cohort who brought their guitar.
There are seven people in my cohort and each of us ended up here with one kinda random but it turns out pretty useful thing. We don't know each other's names. We mostly call each other by the thing we brought with us, so Guitar loaned me their guitar today and so I wrote this song.

I'm going to play it for you now,
in this letter which is happening now,
and then I'm going to go to bed.

I have a big day tomorrow.

[The Novice sings:]

And then
everything went off
and it was so nice

All the lights
all the power
just for a minute
and it was so nice

And then a dog barked
and then a star
and then I thought of you
just for a minute
and it was so nice

[*The Artist joins the Novice singing.*]

And then
everything went off
and it was so nice

All the lights
all the power
just for a minute
and it was so nice

And then a dog barked
and then a star
and then I thought of you
just for a minute
and it was so nice

Dear Dan,
Goodnight.

Okay, so now we're going to skip
Part Two, Part Four, which is called
Exodus, or
Sorry to See You Escar-Go,
and basically what happens in that section is that the cohort
(refer to all gathered)
leaves the asterism—
We all get blown apart, and shipped back in reverse, particle
by sparkling particle, back to the planet Earth
where we're tasked
with enacting
the bright future.
So we're just gonna—
Yeah—
We're just gonna go straight to that.

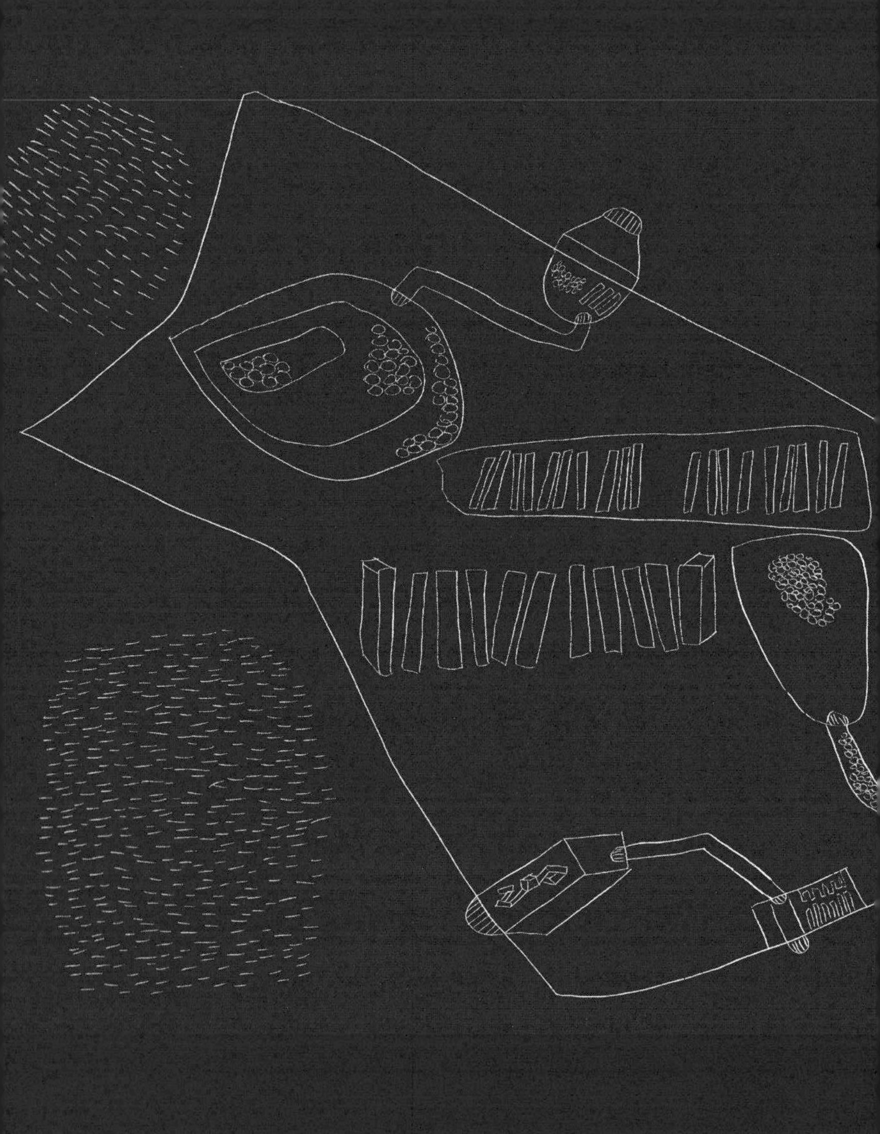

Part Three

The Bright Future

In the Bright Future
you rise up.

You rise and the lights come on.
You do not retaliate or fall into hysterics, you simply rise
and the lights come on.

The door between you
and the outside world opens.
The door between you, the dreamer, and the outside world
opens. The lights come on, the door opens, and you rise.
You do not fall into hysterics.
You do not retaliate.
Of course you will want to run screaming, but you won't.
In the Bright Future, you will not run screaming
every time you want to run screaming.

In the Bright Future,
long after your train has derailed,
after you fell and the lights went off,
after your country, poised to retaliate did not retaliate and after
its citizens
did not fall into hysterics, the lights come on, and you rise.

The door between you, the dreamer, and the outside world
opens and you exit and enter
the Bright Future, where three clouds on their way to the ocean
notice a boat that is headed for some danger. In the Bright
Future, those clouds will point that boat to safety. We
will point each other to safety.

In the Bright Future, the environmental rampage will have ended, amnesty will be given to all those who return to their senses, and it will be said, We are not free yet, but we are on our way! We will find that gentleman who has been struggling on that road with his horse. We will find him, go to him, and offer him assistance.

In the Bright Future, the blockades will be removed, the bridges will uncollapse, and the mud will slide back up the mountain. There will be a word in every language for "to sit outside on a sunny day enjoying a beer."

In the Bright Future, people will say, We are the winners of this round of elections, without any doubt. People will say, You are the winners of this round of elections, without any doubt. There will be fewer head wounds, generally. We cannot eliminate them entirely but we will significantly reduce the number. A loss of three will not be met by a forced gain of one hundred, and when you cry, your boss will cry with you.

In the Bright Future, helicopters will drop flyers in your neighborhood that say YOU ARE WELCOME HERE,
and politicians will leave you voicemails reminding you to pick up toilet paper and tampons. Kindergartens will never be on fire, and babies will never be in the news. Ever! The universal shame will pass, and the tall people will stand in back at the shows. We will all know which situations need to be handled immediately and which are worth putting off. We will not have to struggle with our bearings, and we will not have to fight for our positions. In the Bright Future, we have already survived.
We do not get away from the ugly world,
and we do not get away from the beautiful world, and we no longer need to. We will forge our soft metals into effective, possibly invisible weapons that we will wield
with tremendous acumen.

In the Bright Future, what has been taken will be given back, and reports and reality will be the same. Reports and reality will be the same! There will be candlelight vigils when people die of natural causes, and airplanes will stay in the sky or they won't take off. Extremists, under cover of darkness, will visit neighboring countries and surprise them by wrapping their capital buildings in fairy lights, scattering their fields with wildflower seeds, and leaving poems of towering importance in every mailbox.
Eye contact will be possible.
Also grieving.

In the Bright Future, signs that read, The food we serve here was actually prepared by a person and the ingredients actually came from somewhere will be unnecessary! Signs that read, The food we serve here was actually prepared by a person and the ingredients actually came from somewhere will be obsolete.

And no one will ever lose their right to be here. We will know how to open the windows and doors, when to open the windows and doors, and the dancers, for the most part black boys, will be a bright spark in the day, a moment of unregulated beauty. The word unregulated will occur in the mind of everyone all at once, and everyone here, and everyone there, and everyone everywhere where black boys are dancing will give the black boys a standing ovation.

In the Bright Future, I
will protect you,
and you
will protect me.
I
will protect you,
and you
will protect me. You
will protect them, and they
will protect you. They
will protect us, and we
will protect them. They
will protect you, and you
will protect them. We
will protect them, and they

will protect us.

Nine-year-old girls will have no interest in learning to fire an Uzi. Nine-year-old boys will have no interest in learning to fire an Uzi. Nine-year-old children will have no interest in learning to fire an Uzi. Or no. There will be no Uzis in the Bright Future. You will know that you are a significance, that you are a meaning of beauty, and you will not understand the word Uzi, you will never have heard the word Uzi.

In the Bright Future, teams of experts will be deployed to crown coffee maidens with garlands of flowers, teams of experts will be deployed to give massages to mechanics and road crews, babysitters, groundskeepers, repair people, teachers, bus drivers, toll booth operators, cashiers, bar backs, janitors, window washers, foresters, social workers, and firefighters. We will all be deployed to bring lasagnas to fire stations, and send lasagnas to space stations, and make lasagnas for homeless queer youth.

The mayor will run on a platform of hospitality convenings, she will run on a platform of annual food things, in places that have beds and kitchens in the same physical buildings and also backyards or access to backyards. There will be eating, sleeping in tents, and sharing. She will run on this platform and she will win, and there will be punk rock and soul music in abundance. There will be secret towns and tender cities with galleries of flora. Gardens and poetry will be decriminalized and photojournalism will reveal: People take naps! People hold hands! People simmer lentils! People sit on grass under trees! Public transportation is mostly effectual!

People will wander from one tender city to another. They will borrow and trade and strike up new friendships and this will not have the effect of homogenizing but will have the effect of heartening. In general we will be better passengers.

In the Bright Future, your god and my god walk into a bar on a blind date, and my god blows your god's mind and vice versa. You will not accept circumstances for yourself that you would not wish upon another and vice versa. The ongoing nightmare that the administration has permitted and perpetuated in your department will at last have come to an end. In the Bright Future, your worst nightmare is behind you. Again.
Our worst nightmare is behind us. Again.

And everyone will come home.

Everyone will come home and everyone's home will have everyone's dream kitchen and in everyone's dream kitchen will be everyone's dream cake and everyone will have their dream cake and everyone will eat it too and everyone will have a kitchen or access to a kitchen. We will go to places just to be near people who are special to us, and people won't say, Let me know if you need anything if they don't have anything to offer. Your body will be a mini-kingdom. Your body will be a mini-kingdom. Your body will be a mini-kingdom, and you, its only sovereign.

At a certain point, someone will say, Is this a utopian communal hippie enclave? And someone will answer, Depends. What do you mean by "enclave"?

In the Bright Future, we will not despair when there is conflict. We will not despair for long when there is conflict. Blind spots will not be removed entirely but will regularly and repeatedly be flooded with light. Barriers to perception will even if only fleetingly be removed. People will be like, Wait a minute. What just happened? What did I just see? Did I just see more? The corners of our eyes will expand by degrees, and the suicide rate of black men in this country will continue its downward trend. The suicide rate of transgender people in this country will begin its downward trend. The incarceration rate of black and brown people in this country will begin its downward trend. Or no. There will be no suicide. There will be no incarceration in the Bright Future. You will know that you are a significance, that you are a meaning of beauty, and you will not understand the word suicide, you will never have heard the word incarceration.

There will be sympathy, pitching and swaying, and we'll be able to do everything we currently shy away from. Our skin will vibrate, our cells will vibrate, in anticipation of meeting the persons of our dreams. Our cells will vibrate when we meet the persons of our dreams and we will know we are not dreaming. The Bright Future will be literary, not literal. Or no. The Bright Future will be literary, and literal. And we will be legible in our own languages.

In the Bright Future, thirty-five horses will gather in a field. Lightning! Stars! The sea! Thirty-five horses will gallop toward you, glittering, in the manner of violets coming to light in early spring! We will emerge into some new phase of the human story where the human is sharing the story with other species. We will remember every day that we are very new inhabitants of this planet Earth. Humans are very new inhabitants
of this planet Earth.

In the Bright Future, when the power goes out, we will not panic. We will trust, and we will wait, together,
in the dark, the quiet, the wind, the trees, the light in the sky.
We will not be raised to expect so little of men.

And we will not carry everything with us. We cannot carry everything with us. The caricature of fragile, mid-century, white, American womanhood taken to its hapless and helpless extremes will be abandoned. The crimes of enforced and binary gender and compulsory heterosexuality that hobble our imaginations and our lives will no longer go unpunished. And everything won't seem so just a little bit awful.

We'll learn to eat again. To sleep. To sleep alone. We'll learn to sleep alone again in the middle of the bed.
Some of us will learn how to take up space, and some of us will learn how to make space, how to leave space, how to move over. Some of us will learn both, and the controversy over what part of the body we think with will be resolved.

In the Bright Future, I'll see you again.
I'll see you again in the Bright Future.

I may not see you again, but hopefully I'll see you again
in the Bright Future.

The city is better when you are in it.

The city is better when you are in it.

The city is better
when you are in it.

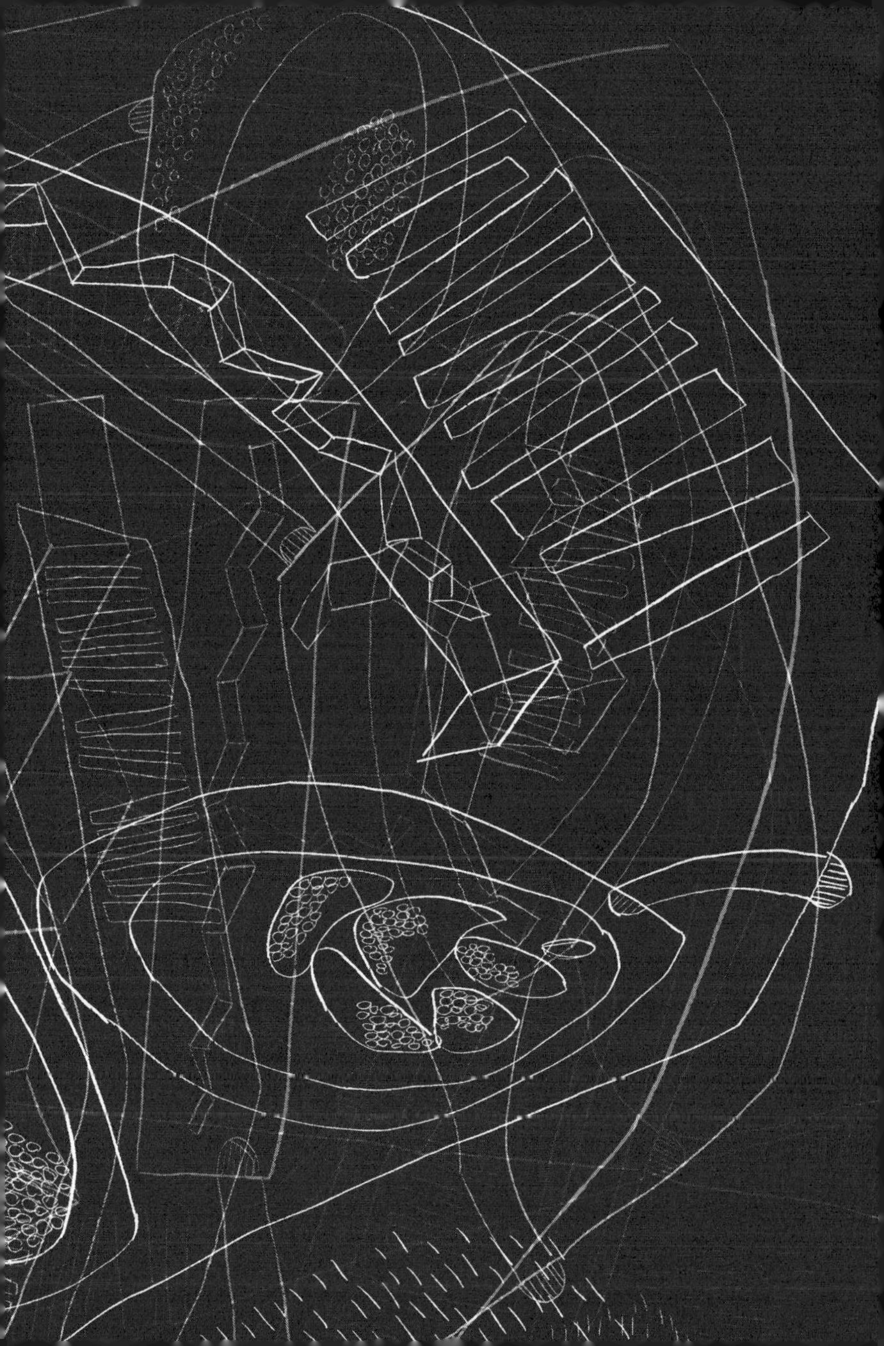

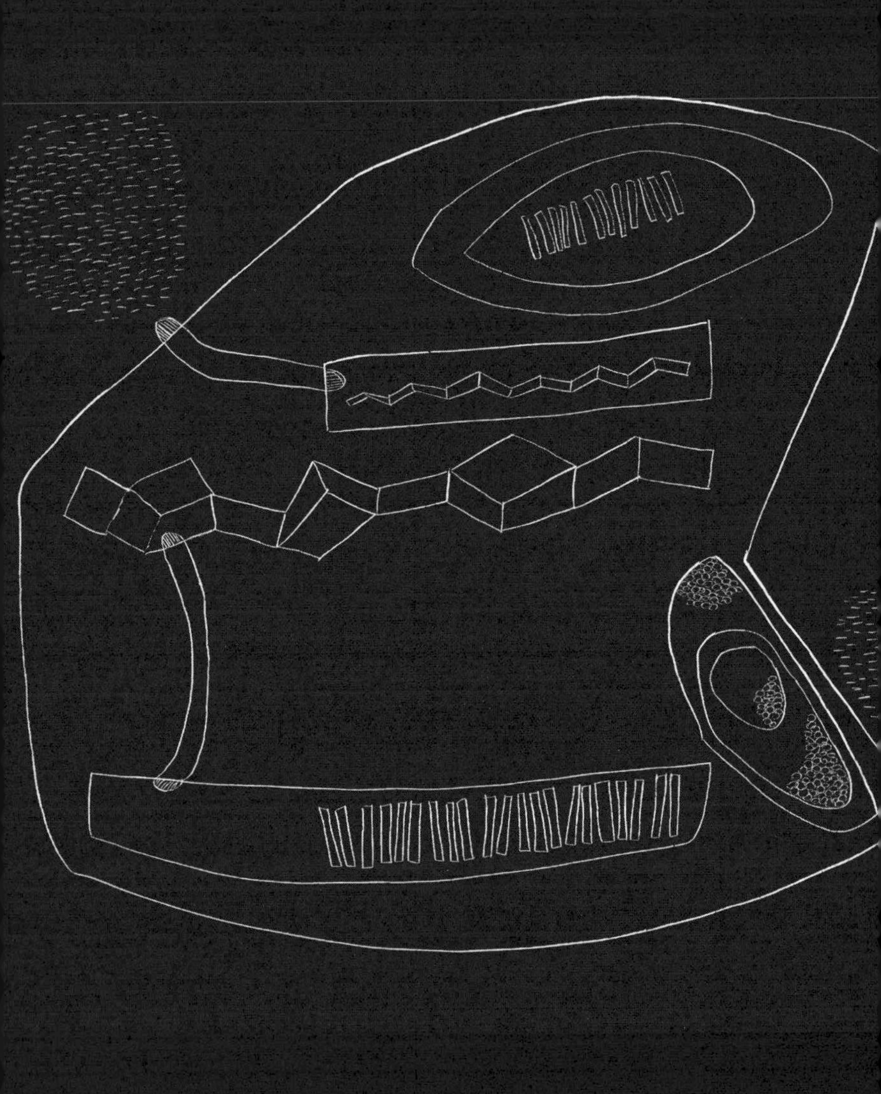

Sources

p. 42 The phrase, "The future will be confusing" is from Tim Etchells's *Will Be, 2010, Two Part Neon Sign* (1999).

p. 82: The image of wrapping buildings in fairy lights is from Tim Etchells's *Certain Fragments*:

> Steve died along with his partner Mark of AIDS-related illnesses in 1988, and his own practice as an editor and writer engaged in a community of artists set a better example than one could reasonably wish for. He told me one day about wanting to do an art project wrapping buildings in fairy lights. I wish I could do that for him now.

p. 83: The phrase, "And the dancers, for the most part black boys, will be a bright spark in the day, a moment of unregulated beauty," is from Teju Cole's essay, "Black Body: Rereading James Baldwin's 'Stranger in the Village'" (2014).

p. 88: The phrases, "The caricature of fragile, mid-century, white, American womanhood taken to its hapless and helpless extremes" and "The crimes of enforced and binary gender and compulsory heterosexuality that hobble our imaginations and our lives" are from Jill Dolan's *Theatre & Sexuality* (2010).

Acknowledgments

In addition to everyone named in the preface, this work would not have been possible without the support and encouragement of Lane Czaplinski, Vallejo Gantner, and Brian Rogers, all of whom extended incredible faith in and patience with me as this project came into being and evolved over the years. Also Matthew Fisher, Maya Kozarski, and Evan Martin who participated in a developmental workshop of this piece during their time as students at Whitman College. And finally, Teresa Guard, Pamm Hanson and Alexis Kane, Heather Kravas, Fox Whitney and Will Courtney, Meredith Clark, Carol Brown, Jeff and Judy Stuhmer, Alyza DelPan-Monley, Elizabeth Duffell, and M Acuff, all of whom hosted the work in their beautiful homes, as well as the good people at the Phinney Neighborhood Association who gave us space to share the work in their busy and buzzy facility. I can't thank you all enough.

Contributors

Kristen Kosmas makes contemporary performance. Her primary materials and concerns are language, presence, liveness, and collaboration with other artists, audiences, and the space, environment, or site she's working in/on. Kosmas has had new works commissioned by the Chocolate Factory (NYC), On the Boards (Seattle), Performance Space 122 (NYC), The Theatre of a Two-Headed Calf (NYC), Seattle University's SITE Specific, Dixon Place (NYC), and the New City Theater in Seattle. Her plays and critically acclaimed solo performances have been presented in Seattle, Austin, Boston, Chicago, Los Angeles, and in New York City at numerous venues including the Chocolate Factory, PS 122, La Mama, Dixon Place, Prelude, Barbès, the Ontological/Hysteric Downstairs Series, and the Poetry Project. Her writing has been published by Ugly Duckling Presse, PLAY: A Journal of Plays, and 53rd State Press, among others. Kosmas is a founding member of the OBIE Award-winning performance series Little Theater (NYC); The Twenty-Five Cent Opera of San Francisco, a monthly event for the enactment of texts and theatricals (NYC); Birthday Girl, a nomadic celebration of new performance in Seattle; and Machiqq (aka The Ladies Auxilliary Playwriting Team), a non-geographically bound women's experimental writing collective.

Leon Finley is a trans, interdisciplinary artist born in Seattle, WA in 1987. His work crosses over performance, sculpture and drawing and comes out of his experiences having a physical and spiritual body. His work is concerned with interdependency: the relationships between all kinds of bodies (human, animal, plant, object, architecture, sound, etc.) and the idea that bodies are vibrating, that matter is not solid but is, in fact, moving, permeable and changeable. Leon received his BFA from Cooper Union in 2009 and his MFA in Sculpture from Yale in 2012. Leon was the recipient of the Jacques and Natasha Gelman Trust Prize in 2009, the Blair Dickinson Memorial Prize, the Dan David Prize Scholarship in 2012, and was a finalist for The Henry Art Gallery Brink Award in 2017. Leon has shown work around New York and Seattle including galleries such as The Alice and the Jacob Lawrence gallery and has performed in venues such as the Whitney Museum of American Art as a part of Kevin Beasley's Public Programs in Sonic Masses and Movement Research as a part of the Open Performance Series. Leon has taught at Cooper Union, Virginia Commonwealth University and Montclair State University. He currently lives and works in Seattle, Washington.

Daniel Alexander Jones's wildflower body of work grows in relationship to a wide range of audiences. *Black Light* premiered at the Public Theater/Joe's Pub for a critically acclaimed 6-week run. *Duat* premiered at Soho Rep in 2016. His other performance pieces and plays include *Radiate*, *Phoenix Fabrik*, *Blood:Shock:Boogie*, and *Bel Canto, The Book of Daniel*, made with musician Walter Kitundu and director Tea Alagic. Daniel was named a 2019 Guggenheim Fellow and a 2015 Doris Duke Artist in recognition of his risk-taking practice.

Book design + layout: Kate Kremer
Cover image + interior cartography: Leon Finley
Cover design: Jonathan Crimmins

53rd State Press publishes lucid, challenging, and lively new writing for performance. Our catalog includes new plays as well as scores and notations for interdisciplinary performance, graphic adaptations, and essays on theater and dance. The press was founded in 2007.

For more info or to order books, please visit 53rdstatepress.org.

53rd State Press books are available to the trade through TCG (Theater Communications Group) and are distributed by Consortium: https://cbsd.com.

The People's Republic of Valerie, Living Room Edition is made possible by the New York State Council on the Arts with the support of Governor Andrew M. Cuomo and the New York State Legislature.

Also from 53rd State Press:

The Book of the Dog // Karinne Keithley
Joyce Cho Plays // Joyce Cho
No Dice // Nature Theater of Oklahoma
When You Rise Up // Miguel Gutierrez
Montgomery Park, or Opulence // Karinne Keithley
Crime or Emergency // Sibyl Kempson
Off the Hozzle // Rob Erickson
A Map of Virtue + Black Cat Lost // Erin Courtney
Pig Iron: Three Plays // Pig Iron Theatre Company
The Mayor of Baltimore + Anthem // Kristen Kosmas
Ich, Kürbisgeist + The Secret Death of Puppets // Sibyl Kempson
Soulographie: Our Genocides // Erik Ehn
Life and Times: Episode 1 // Nature Theater of Oklahoma
Life and Times: Episode 2 // Nature Theater of Oklahoma
Life and Times: Episodes 3 + 4 // Nature Theater of Oklahoma
The 53rd State Occasional No. 1 // Ed. Paul Lazar
There There // Kristen Kosmas
Seagull (Thinking of You) // Tina Satter
Self Made Man Man Made Land // Ursula Eagly
Another Telepathic Thing // Big Dance Theater
Another Tree Dance // Karinne Keithley Syers
Let Us Now Praise Susan Sontag // Sibyl Kempson
Dance by Letter // Annie-B Parson
Pop Star Series // Neal Medlyn
The Javier Plays // Carlos Murillo
Minor Theater: Three Plays // Julia Jarcho
Ghost Rings (12-inch vinyl) // Half Straddle
A New Practical Guide to Rhetorical Gesture and Action // NTUSA
A Field Guide to iLANDing // iLAND
The 53rd State Occasional No. 2 // Ed. Will Arbery
Suicide Forest // Kristine Haruna Lee
Rude Mechs' Lipstick Traces // Lana Lesley + the Rude Mechs
A Discourse on Method // Shonni Enelow + David Levine
MILTON // PearlDamour

Forthcoming:

WATER SPORTS; or insignificant white boys // Jeremy O. Harris
Wood Calls Out to Wood // Corinne Donly
I Understand Everything Better // David Neumann + Sibyl Kempson
ASTRS // Karinne Keithley Syers
Best Behavior // David Levine
Severed // Ignacio Lopez
Ann, Fran, and Mary Ann // Erin Courtney
12 Shouts to the Ten Forgotten Heavens // Sibyl Kempson